Thoughts and Feelings

(An Anthology of Poems)

Audrey Donoghue

Contents

That's What Friends Are For

She stares through her window as we all pass by,
We give her a wave and mouth the word 'Hi'.
Her windows unwashed and her curtains threadbare,
She looks so unhappy, doesn't anyone care.

As we stroll past the house the very next day,
No face at the window fills us with dismay.
We'll knock on her door on the way home from work,
From this resolution we resolved not to shirk.

As we walk up the path there's weeds in galore,
No-one seems around so Dave kicks in the door.
We find a frail figure huddled up on the bed,
She's barely alive, unwashed and unfed.

We light a big fire and brew a pot of tea,
She now looks a bit better on that we agree.
We make her a hot meal and clean through her house,
We tidy her garden with never a grouse.

This fragile old lady wipes a tear from her eye,
As she thanks us profusely and gives a big sigh.
"I'm so very grateful for all you have done,
I've no one to care now I've lost my dear son."

"We'll all be your children and call twice a week,
You've been an inspiration, helped us become meek.
We'll tidy your garden and wash, clean and cook,
That's what friends are for, you relax with a book."

Winner 'Pontypool Poetry Competition' 2009.

The Joys of Friendship

Friendship is the most wonderful treasure,
The joy it brings is beyond all measure.
In times of trouble when one feels so poor,
You turn to your friends, that's what friends are for.

Baby Josh clasps his mother's thumb in a firm grip,
As he nestles in her arms against her silky slip.
Secure and well loved his gaze begins to wander,
Seeking friendships from his family and yonder.

Happy at school he makes a very special friend,
With whom he has fun and also learns to lend.
His fortune now changes and he has his first fight,
With a black eye and torn jeans he looks a real sight.

Growing up too quickly he enters his teens,
Most parents will understand just what that means.
Friendship at this age means loud music and girls,
Some of his antics make his parents' hair curl.

After playing the field he makes friends with Jill,
Enamoured, he proposes and she says "I will".
Their marriage is blessed with a girl and twin boys,
So their orderly home is now littered with toys.

They have some broken nights causing lack of sleep,
And sometimes Jill breaks down and has a good weep.
Next morning they rise and look at their brood,
They acknowledge their luck and feel in a good mood.

As their family grow up friends come and go,
They have many encounters, some high and some low.
They share with each other and give so much more,
And are happy to admit, without friends they'd be poor.

The Price

There's a price to pay for being alive,
In spite of the pleasure that we all derive.
There's pain, sleepless nights and a long weary fight,
When troubles and trials creep up overnight.

There's a price to pay for taking one's pleasure,
Not thinking of others, hell bent on all leisure.
When the good times have past and the barrel's run dry,
One regrets one's past actions, tries hard not to cry.

There's a price to pay for that innocence lost,
Never stopping to think what would be the cost.
Life looked at no longer through rose coloured glasses,
With eyes opened wide life's bliss simply passes.

There's a price to pay for that long love affair,
That real close allegiance makes one more aware,
Of the day when the partnership ends for all time,
Then one wishes for days that were once so sublime.

Fourth Prize, National Poetry Competition 1997

Happiness

The first white snowdrops peeping through the ground,
A baby asleep, not making a sound.
Happiness comes from such small, simple things,
They make your heart soar and fly on a wing.

Happiness is a fleeting emotion,
Why we're happy we may have no notion.
Maybe 'twas the feel of warm summer sun,
Making us believe life can be full of fun.

Happiness comes at times unexpected,
Making one smile at thoughts resurrected,
Honeysuckle scent 'long a country lane,
Through all life's woes these memories remain.

A shaft of sunlight shining through woodland trees,
A carpet of bluebells, swaying in the breeze.
Such sights give happiness beyond compare,
Spurs one on to preserve life, try more to care.

The Secret of a Happy Life

I wander as a lonely soul,
Life's not much fun when on the dole.
No work to fill my empty day,
No mates to help me on my way

I stay in bed till half-past three,
Not needed now, I'm fancy free.
I do some shopping for my Nan,
She helps me feel I'm still a man.

I arrive back home, the postman's been,
The biggest post I've ever seen.
Two firms require me for a job,
At last a chance to earn a bob.

Next morning I awake at six,
I catch the bus, with people mix.
My head held high, I feel so proud,
'Life's good again,' I cry out loud.

My job is hard, the hours long,
My body aches, I'm not so strong.
Works not all it's cracked up to be,
I'm thinking now it's not for me.

I hurry home and pack my bags,
Pants, socks and shirts and twenty fags.
I hit the road, a tramp I'll be,
And live my life down by the sea.

The Vagrant

He tramps o'er vale and countryside,
He may be poor but has his pride.
His worldly goods upon his back
Carried in an old worn sack.

Nuts and berries form his banquet,
The stars at night act as a blanket.
No alarm to wake him in the morn,
The cockerel does the job at dawn.

He doesn't have a grand position,
He's broken faith with all tradition.
He'll beg and steal from where he can,
And wonder how it all began.

He looks back on his early life,
His home was full of hate and strife,
And on reflection he can see,
That at long last he now is free.

The Seasons

Spring, a time of all rebirth,
When life bursts forth with all her worth.
Birds build their nests, they hope unseen,
Whilst trees await their summer screen.

Summer sun makes all things blossom,
Brooks babble on and carry flotsam.
Butterflies unfold their wings,
Such happiness the sunshine brings.

Autumn leaves of red and yellow,
The sun alas begins to mellow,
Birds gather for their yearly flight,
To distant lands by day and night.

Winter time the trees are bare,
Snow, ice and frost make us aware,
Of icicles hung from telephone wires,
And roasting chestnuts on big log fires.

Winter Scenes

Leaves of every colour dancing wildly in the gale,
Twisting, twirling, huddling close against the stony hail.
Summer flowers now resting, all beaten by the rain,
Awaiting resurrection, when life bursts forth again.

Holly trees fully laden with berries ripe and red,
Brightening up the landscape, defying all things dead.
Bramblings fly in from the North, inhabiting our wood,
Heralding the winter, flaunting plumage bright and good.

Hoar frosts embroider gardens with threads of finest lace,
Embellishing the flowers with beauty and with grace.
Robins guard their territory, like sentries on parade,
Making the mid-winter scene a wonderful charade.

Reflections of the trees make patterns on the snow,
The skyline clear of life but for a solitary crow.
The virgin snow as yet untrod lays thick upon the ground,
The winter scene is one of peace until vibrant spring comes round.

The Joys of Spring

Spring has greeted us once again.
The long, dark winter has departed.
Young lovers hold hands and enjoy the warm sunshine.
Old men smile and reflect on their youth,
As real and imaginary lovers are resurrected and memories
evoked.
Clumps of pure white snowdrops herald the awakening of
springtime.
Shy violets peep through the hedgerows, vying for attention with
beautiful, yellow primroses.
The hedgerows are bursting with buds, ready to open and give
shelter to birds and insects.
Cherry trees flaunt their spring blossom, floating down in the
breeze,
Covering the drab earth with a beautiful, pink carpet.
Enchanting catkins dangle and shake on the hazel tree,
As they await a visit from the busy bee.
Some, unable to wait, fall into the nearby swollen river.
Approaching Welsh towns, displays of stately daffodils nod and
dance,
Lifting the spirits of passing travellers.
In the fields, black and white new born lambs gamble and frolic,
Just a short distance from their patient, long suffering mothers.
Country dwellers are treated to a free orchestral concert,
As our feathered friends give a rendition of their delightful 'Dawn
Chorus'.
How lucky we are to have the spring, when life is rekindled,
refreshing our tired and jaded souls,
And giving us hope for a brighter future.

The Dark Valley

I live in a valley of darkness and fear,
My life appears empty without any cheer.
No worldly possession will lift my 'Black Dog',
Can't see my way forward, I'm blinded by fog

If only the sun would shine down on me,
I'd rise up and embrace it and set myself free,
To start my time over, re-evaluate my life,
Work hard, avoid pitfalls and stay clear of strife.

My new medication is starting to work,
I'm feeling much better, it is a real perk,
I'm climbing out of the valley and into the light,
I feel like an eagle about to take flight.

The valley's behind me, I'm scaling the mountain,
I'm thirsty for life as I drink from the fountain.
I envisage a life full of laughter and fun,
The past is behind me, I now see the sun.

Envy

Envy is a horrendous evil,
An appetite like a full blown weevil,
Destroying people, lands and countries,
In pursuit of larger, endless bounties.

Envy makes our children spiteful,
Without this vice they'd be delightful.
Think of the child, who seems to have all,
Envy prevents her having a ball.

Envy sends our precious sons to war,
Making our lives so very poor.
What's gained by a piece of land newly won,
Compared with the loss of an innocent son.

Envy destroys minds that once were so pure,
By wishing for all things that allure.
Don't envy, aim for that bright distant star,
That way you'll prosper and also head far.

The Mystery of Love

Why do you love me I asked my sweet Grace?
I listened intently as I searched her dear face.
"It's a question I've given much thought" she replied,
"I've still no idea though I've searched high and wide.

Why does the sun rise each day and set every night,
Giving us darkness and also daylight.
And why does the tide ebb and flow every day,
As it lashes 'gainst rocks in our beautiful bays.

Why does an acorn grow into a tree?
Giving shelter and beauty for all folk to see.
Why are we born to face struggle and strife?
These questions need answers to the meaning of life.

Life is a mystery of which love forms a part,
Man has tried hard to understand right from the start.
But one thing I know Bill my love will not die."
I looked at sweet Grace and gave a big sigh.

Sounds I Love

I love the sound of church bells ringing,
Melodic sound of choirboys singing,
Making Sunday such a special day,
Chasing our cares and worries away.

I love the sound of raindrops falling,
On dry, parched earth and dry stone walling,
Refreshing all the garden flowers,
By nature's own amazing powers.

I love the sound of a babbling brook,
I'm drawn to its banks to take a look.
Pure spring water laps o'er pebble stones,
Creating music of many tones.

I love the sound of a humming bee,
As I sunbathe in the luscious lea.
He flits 'round plants collecting honey,
Enjoyed on picnics when it's sunny.

Living Near a Wood

As I contemplate the trees,
I find myself drawn more to thee.
As thoughts pass through my troubled mind,
I find myself start to unwind.

A wood is home to many creatures,
Which makes it a delightful feature,
And gives me many hours of pleasure,
To fill my life in times of leisure.

The sweetness of the birds' 'Dawn Chorus',
An orchestra played solely for us,
Never fails to lift my spirits,
And all life's cares elope 'long with it.

The squirrel's antics, so amusing,
Leaping, flying, daily storing.
Summer's sun will soon be gone,
Another year rolling on.

Now I'm in my Golden Years,
Woodland pleasures erode my fears.
From buds in May till late November,
Young fires aflame to passing embers.

A Country Walk

I like to take a nice long walk,
And think, revise and sometimes talk,
To folk I meet upon the way,
We smile and pass the time of day.

Proud owners with their dogs pass by,
And sometimes I just wonder why,
Of all the forms of life there are,
Man's best friend is the dog, by far.

My walk progresses through the valley,
Now and then I have to dally,
To rest upon the springy pasture,
Nature's joys make me enrapture.

I walk on to the little stream,
The hypnotic water makes me dream,
Of other lands and times gone by,
I sit entranced and give a sigh.

My walk is nearly at its end,
My spirit now is sure to mend.
I'll work all through the coming week,
With thoughts of future walks, my peak.

Llantarnam

Llantarnam, a place abounding with history,
An Abbey and Church creating some mystery.
With a fine Comprehensive and Industrial Park,
Llantarnam is thriving and making its mark.

The life of the Abbey dates back hundreds of years,
Seen Kings come and go and witnessed many fears.
Given to the 'White Monks' in Eleven Seventy Nine,
Is now home to forty nuns who are coping just fine.

In St. Michael's church yard lies John Fielding, so brave,
Acknowledged each year by wreaths laid on his grave.
He won the Victoria Cross for his valiant acts,
Recorded in history books with all of the facts.

Next to the Church is the friendly 'Greenhouse' Inn,
Where a drink can be enjoyed along with your kin.
Weddings and funerals all congregate here,
Conversation flows freely helped along by the beer.

Abergavenny

Abergavenny, Y fenni, that fine market town,
Where all can be purchased, from a pig to a gown.
Situated at the foot of the great Skirrid mountain,
A day out to compare with Rome's Trevi Fountain.

The shops are unique and some are quite classy,
They appeal to all ages and that trendy wee lassie.
All can be found without walking too far,
And when one gets tired there's some excellent bars.

At the back of the shops, there's a lovely old park,
Where families go when the kids want to lark.
There's swings, playing fields and a lovely landscape,
Where happy times can be spent, when one needs to escape.

Market day's on a Tuesday, best day of the week,
They come from near and afar, their fortunes to seek.
The farmers come in with their cattle to sell,
Whilst their wives sell their produce, a job they do well.

With a market, castle and river, Y fenni's the tops,
And people all come and shop till they drop.
They travel by bus, coach and even by train,
And nought puts them off, not even the rain.

Growing Up in Pontnewydd

When we were young we had no restrictions,
Some things that we did were beyond description.
We skated on the iced canal at 'Five Locks',
More often than not went home with wet socks.

On hot days we swam down Cwmbran Clayhole,
Diving from 'The Rock' was always our main goal.
On the way home we bought chips from Kelly's shop,
Which we ate and washed down with bottles of pop.

At 'Church School' break time, we played many good games,
Before 'Political Correctness', we all had nick names.
We played hop-skotch, skipping and sometimes rounders,
We cheated and fell out, we really were bounders.

A walk to Twm Barlwm we'd go on warm days,
We'd stroll up 'The Incline', watching cattle graze.
At the top of the pimple we'd sit down and eat,
On the long journey back we were always dead beat.

'The White Rose' cinema was our Saturday treat,
A penny was all we paid for our seat.
As the cavalry charged we shouted and cheered,
The Indians may not be beaten we feared.

Sunday was the one day we had to conform,
Washed and brushed up we tried to reform.
Off to chapel or church for afternoon school,
Welsh children were required to obey this rule.

The Mature Student

He peeps around the door of the long dreaded class.
He called at the pub first to down a few bass,
To give himself courage to face the ordeal,
To read and to write has long been his ideal.

A young girl comes forward with long flowing hair,
She puts him at ease and gives him a chair.
"Sit yourself down, once we all felt the same,
But now we're all reading and writing our name."

Introductions are made and a tutor is found,
He commences lessons with his head to the ground.
As they work together his confidence grows,
His writing improves and his reading now flows.

Twelve months go by and he enters the class,
His face is now beaming, no need of the bass.
He's helping his son now, whose reading was poor,
And seeking advancement through a new open door.

A Broken Romance

This life that's inside me, my one reason to care,
I should feel so happy but just feel despair.
I just cared too much, I'm not really bad,
Why was I reckless?   I must have been mad.

I remember his face and his handsome good looks,
His knowledge of music and his hunger for books.
He swept me along on a tide of romance,
With my naïve sweet nature I hadn't a chance.

He dined me and wined me and courted me well,
My family and friends said they heard wedding bells.
He took me to meet his mum and his dad,
The way it's turned out is so very sad.

I thought that he loved me and our future was sure,
But now I can see that his love was not pure.
From the moment I told him we were to be three,
He broke my poor heart and gave me back the key.

The Corner Shop

The floor has been swept, the sawdust all scattered,
Flowers put in a bucket, some looking quite battered.
The first customer enters with her usual request,
"Two streaky pieces for Jim and a pound of the best."

My parents worked real hard till eleven at night,
Money was short and budgets were tight.
No money to spend on freezers and fridges,
Cold slabs and white netting kept off the midges.

We lived two up, two down, at the back of the shop,
Along with the stock and a few crates of pop.
Mam used up the old veg and bruised apples for dinner,
Dad must have considered he'd married a winner.

Few customers paid fully for their goods with hard cash,
The thought of so doing brought some out in a rash.
A few bob off the slate was the most some could pay,
With the promise of more on some other day.

The Sunday School Outing

The Sunday School outing at last has arrived,
For month after month everyone has contrived,
To make this day out the finest one ever,
They worked long and hard towards this endeavour.

The bus has arrived, the driver is seated,
The children get on, everyone warmly greeted.
The journey this year is a trip to the seaside,
They hope to arrive in time for a full tide.

The sea has been spotted, they all give a cheer,
They get off the bus all carrying their gear.
They head for the beach with their buckets and spades,
The Head leads the group carrying two, huge sun-shades.

The beach looks inviting, the water is clear,
The children rush forward without any fear.
Costumes are put on and castles are built,
They eat, drink and have fun without any guilt.

The day is now ended, they stroll to the bus,
Happy and contented, no-one makes a fuss.
They sing and tell old jokes to their hearts' content,
And recall their great outing and how the day went.

The Miner

The miner returns from his shift at the pit.
He works really hard doing his little bit,
From seven in the morning, till seven at night.
Working like that can never be right.

He bathes in a tin bath in front of the fire,
And looks at his furniture which is mostly on hire.
He tries to relax, singing songs for the chapel,
But his son puts him off loudly crunching an apple.

His wife dries his back with a big coloured towel,
She loves her strong man from the pit of her bowels.
She's cooked him a hot meal, a lovely rich stew,
Followed much later by his favourite brew.

His mates have arrived to go to the choir,
Of these yearly concerts they never do tire.
The singing was fine, the audience lost,
They wrap up real good to go out in the frost.

They arrive home at last, there's no doors to lock,
Possessions are few in this little block.
Friendships are true and everything's shared more,
The young and the old are all fully cared for.

The Bride

The bride has arrived in a pony and trap,
She's trying really hard not to get in a flap.
She walks down the aisle on the arm of her dad,
He's loved her so much, deep down he feels sad.

The organ is playing, Aunt Mary is weeping,
A hush fills the church as the vicar starts speaking.
Vows are exchanged and rings put on their fingers,
The choir closes the service with well-rehearsed singers.

Outside the church the photographer's ready,
He positions the group holding his camera steady.
Everyone's happy, the tension has lifted,
From the pictures he's taken he's really quite gifted.

On to the reception for a really fine spread,
Everyone's so glad the couple are wed.
The speeches are funny, the wine overflowing,
The bride looks so lovely, she really is glowing.

The wedding is over, the guests have gone home,
The bride and the groom have departed for Rome.
Two weeks in the sun in that romantic city,
Then back to reality, oh what a pity.

The Housewife

The group that surrounds her are all true professionals,
From bankers to lawyers to bright intellectuals.
She'd worried for weeks what to say to them all,
She'd no conversation that she could recall.

She looks back on her life and recalls her day's work,
From seven in the morning and no time to shirk.
She cleans through her house and works out her budget,
With her meagre income there's no way she could fudge it.

She dresses her two children and heads for the shop,
She buys fresh fruit for health, not forgetting the pop.
On the way home her wee son falls on his head,
So he needs a good cuddle and a half day in bed.

The garden's the next chore that needs to be done,
The kids join in the work and they have lots of fun.
It's now time for tea, there's potatoes to peel,
Jane and Sam shell the peas in exchange for a deal.

The deal is for a story about the wicked witch,
Which she reads with expression without hardly a hitch.
Her babes are asleep so she climbs down the stairs,
And rests her poor legs on her favourite chair.

That's an average day in her fulfilling life,
She now looks on her work as worth all the strife.
At last she feels strong and can now hold her own,
So she joins in the talk with a confident tone.

She talks about gardening and trimming the dog,
And of how she's aware she's a very small cog,
In the machine of life to which we all belong,
Some working really hard for only a song.

She's released inhibitions that once held her back,
But now at last she's convinced she's on the right track.
She's made friends with the leader whose nickname is Marty,
And has finally found she's enjoying the party.

Lost Treasure

She spent all her life hunting for treasure,
Her urge to get rich knowing no measure.
She worked long and hard to achieve her aim,
But great wealth she sadly as yet couldn't claim.

Her long search had begun when she was just seven,
Whilst down on vacation in sunny South Devon.
She found a gold locket buried in the sand,
She polished it up till it looked really grand.

All through her childhood she remembered this find,
It had made an impression on her young mind.
The search for more gold or any new treasure,
Took over her life, became her main pleasure.

She spent her teen years pursuing the rich,
But did not account for an arrow to pitch.
It pierced through her heart somewhere from above,
The consequence being she married for love.

Her husband was poor but she loved her dear Tim,
No money to spare, their prospects looked grim.
From nine in the morning till well past midnight,
She worked on her schemes to improve their sad plight.

She was now old and grey and her husband had died,
So she sat in her chair and she cried and she cried,
For all the years wasted spent searching for gold,
The thought of her actions left her feeling quite cold.

Her treasure had been with her, right under her nose,
A treasure as great as her favourite rose.
A vision of Tim appeared before her eyes,
She blew him a kiss as they said their goodbyes.

A pat on the head brought her down to earth,
It was her dear Kate, always full of mirth.
"Come on mum, I'm taking you out for the day",
She looked at her daughter and her tears fell away.

Go Gently

Go gently into that sweet night,
Your work accomplished, you've now earned the right,
To look back on achievements and things you did wrong,
The setbacks, you acknowledge, have made you quite strong.

Go gently into that sweet night,
Your book being published was such a delight.
The shackles of fame soon mar the outer guilding,
Man's true happiness comes whilst he is building.

Go gently into that sweet night,
Your suffering has helped you see the true light.
Family and friends are now your only need,
Love of mankind has become your new creed.

The Wait

How long do I wait to see my Prince Charming?
My patience is short which is quite alarming.
Every day our future I lovingly plan,
As I wash and dust and shop for my Nan.

To help with the war, I join the Red Cross.
I'm good at my job and soon become boss.
We make meals for the needy bombed in the blitz,
And entertain them with folk songs and Liszt.

Time now passes quickly, the wait will be over,
I'll soon be so happy, like walking on clover.
I look forward to the day when I see my sweetheart,
And from that day forward we'll never part.

He's here at last, he's in my arms,
I now feel so happy and completely calm.
I look into his eyes as he fondles my breast,
Then we fall asleep, we need a good rest.

Next morning I wake, glad the waiting is done,
And thank God for the birth of my newly born son.

Life's Challenges

Life is a challenge from beginning to end,
Folk struggle with life as their country they defend.
Babies are born with life's trials to face,
A challenge indeed, whatever their race.

Over 2,000 years ago Christ came to earth,
Jesus has challenged the world since his humble birth.
He tried to turn the world away from sin towards love,
He was sent as a sacrifice by his father above.

Ghandi challenged Gt.Britain for India's 'Home Rule',
The action he took was clever, brave and cool.
This frail, stubborn man was not willing to bend,
By non-violence and starvation he achieved his end.

Martin Luther King had a dream throughout his short life,
To fulfil his dream caused considerable strife.
His challenge was to make black people equal to white,
He gave the black race courage to win the good fight.

Mother Theresa was a nun who worked hard in Calcutta,
Feeding and loving children she found in the gutter.
She met the challenge every day of her life,
To eradicate hunger and poverty which was rife.

The hardest challenge that I've ever known,
Was met by a sweet, plucky girl called Jill Mallone.
She was told she'd be blind by the age of just twenty,
She prepared for this ordeal with knowledge a-plenty.

She stored every colour, scene and face in her vast mind,
She studied animals, birds and flowers of every kind.
She resolved to recall these pictures at a later date,
As she had been handed such a very cruel fate.

At home she closed her eyes and felt her way around,
She tried to be quiet and not make a sound.
She made a cup of tea without spilling a drop,
She cleaned her kitchen floor with water and a mop.

My preconceived view of courage started to crumble,
As this amazing girl made me feel very humble.

The Search for Youth

Since the age of forty you'd longed to be young,
Jane had had a face-lift and its praises she'd sung.
You'd draw out your savings and go under the knife,
You were happy now you knew you'd have a new life.

Your appointment arranged you head to the hospital,
Your surgeon is able and very hospitable.
He's do a nip and a tuck that very same day,
His eyes study your face as he works out his pay.

You wake in the morning your teeth in a mug,
You'd like nothing better than a good hug.
You turn but have a sharp pain in your back,
You scream and cry out, "I've a lumbago attack."

Your face bandaged up, your eyes peering out,
Your lips swollen badly you look like a trout.
Your teeth will not fit right inside your mouth,
Your back is much worse, it's dragging down South.

At home hubby serves you with a drink and a straw,
He's cooked bacon and eggs which look really raw.
"Get out of this room before I throw this tray,"
He quickly retreats only glad to obey.

You shout out, "I'm sorry, please come back in,
I know I've been moody, forgive me my sin.
I won't try to regain my youth anymore,
I'd rather be happy and not such a bore."

An Optimistic Upbringing

From an early age he'd been taught by his dad,
To smile, keep his chin up, try not to be sad.
This lesson had been his guide throughout life,
From his busy school days to choosing his wife.

The marriage had been blessed with three lovely girls,
With great, big blue eyes and a mass of fair curls.
His optimism ensured they had loads of fun,
Spent time swimming, dancing and going for a run.

His life ran smoothly, his marriage was first rate,
He was truly happy, helped by the hand of fate.
When he was forty his life changed for the worse,
It was as if he'd been struck by a strange curse.

He became unemployed, landed up on the dole,
His confidence went, he felt he'd lost his soul.
His marriage collapsed and his future looked grim,
No money to spare, luxuries he had to trim.

He'd now hit rock-bottom, the only way was up,
He remembered dad's advice, bought himself a pup.
His health improved greatly, he found a new job,
He was happy once more, no more reason to sob.

He now knew his father's advice was pure gold,
He ran the rest of his life as he had been told.
He became a true optimist, never got down,
He smiled every day, never displaying a frown.

Running for Gold

I'm up at 5.30 to run my six miles,
I run across country, jumping over stiles.
Muesli for breakfast, then I cycle to work,
I work very hard, there's no time to shirk.

I'm home at 6.30, I eat a light meal,
A few minutes rest I manage to steal,
I then have a cold shower and go to the gym,
Then I fall asleep while watching a film.

That's been my routine for over eight weeks,
I'm trying to get fit so as I reach my peak.
I'm running the mile for the Olympic Games,
And hoping to win and achieve some fame.

The night before the games I go out to dinner,
I eat plenty of carbs so I'll be a winner.
I'm tempted to have some raspberry tart,
But I want to stay lean to make a good start.

The games have begun, I'm running that mile,
I run like a hare showing a good style.
While on the fourth lap I increase my pace,
The cheers are deafening as I win the race.

With my arms in the air I'm shouting and crying,
"I've won mam, I've won, I'm really not lying."
"Whatever's the matter son, were you having a dream?
I warned you last night to lay off that cream.

Glorious Food

Mam's favourite food is fish and chips,
Guaranteed to put pounds on the hips.
She eats them outside in the fresh air,
Where she feels free and without a care.

Dad's quite partial to a nice mixed grill,
But not so keen on paying the bill,
So he rarely goes out for a nosh,
But when he does he dresses up posh.

Grannie loves nothing better than tripe,
Followed by strawberries, fresh and ripe.
She likes to eat sat at the table
Whilst reading facts on the bottle label.

Granddad loves good old sausage and mash,
A good meal to have as he's short of cash.
He eats his meal in front of the telly,
Chomping his food whilst filling his belly.

Teenagers hate traditional meals,
Having to conform just makes them reel.
Teenagers like to go to McDonald's,
Eat burgers, chips and end up at Ronald's.

Life's Journey

Life is like a roundabout,
As it travels round and round.
It starts with birth as life bursts forth,
And ends beneath the earthy ground.

A new born babe gives one new hope,
It's beauty so appealing.
It gives new strength for one to cope,
And life's wounds get new healing.

The child has grown, so strong and bright,
Her dancing brings much pleasure.
She plays and skips till late at night,
Her life is one of leisure.

Childhood now past, still life goes on,
And love enters the picture.
She had a son and called him John,
He grew to be her future.

Life's slipping by, her grandson born,
She sings him nursery rhymes,
And though she's old and frail and worn,
She still enjoys good times.

A Changed Outlook

I turn over in bed, I feel such despair,
My mind feels so numb, I no longer care.
The papers are full of stabbings and bad news,
While strikers insist on airing their views.

The sunlight shines in through a chink in the curtain,
Which alters my viewpoint, I'm now not so certain,
That I should be wallowing here in my bed,
There's breakfast to cook and the cat must be fed.

Breakfast consumed, I head for the garden,
I'll plant those begonias as soon as they harden.
I feel so uplifted, my spirit is rising,
Caring for flowers it's not so surprising.

I now feel so happy, I've worked out a plan,
I'll strive to be better, to become a good man.
I'll answer that ad and join up with 'World Vision',
And hope that one day there'll be a revision.

All men will be equal and acknowledged by all,
Prejudice will die and crime rate will fall
People will be happy and help one another,
The world's population will be like one big brother.

The Magic of Music

If music be the food of love, play on,
It soothes the soul till daily cares are gone.
At the end of the day it provides relaxation,
From the worries of life and endless taxation.

Bach, Beethoven and Mozart, voted top three,
A fine combination I have to agree.
To listen to all three is such a delight,
Lifts downhearted spirits whatever your plight.

Some folk like classical music, others like pop.
Teenagers like pop music to which they can bop.
Their pulsating music sends dad off to the pub,
Where he can relax and be right in the hub.

Music attracts people from many places,
Concerts and festivals unite other races.
Music can talk when language is unknown,
Through such entertainment friendships have grown.

A Cry for The Environment

The environment needs to be tackled worldwide,
By combined work and effort by folk from all sides.
With pollution increasing day after day,
The future looks bleak and full of dismay.

Our high streets are littered and covered in gum,
Spat out by teenagers and an occasional mum.
Fine memorial seats burnt down in the park,
By hooligans who boast, 'It's just for a lark.'

Our rivers are choked with old junk and waste,
Thrown in by folk in too much of a haste.
They say, 'Live for today not for tomorrow',
Whilst those who care deeply are full of real sorrow.

We could all play our part to make our country clean,
Helping hands would work wonders to improve the scene.
Take time to clean up, put litter in the bin,
If we all pull together, I'm sure we could win.

This country would become such a beautiful place,
Make us proud to belong to the human race.
Visitors would enjoy our pristine green land,
And remember our heritage which is really grand.

Love

Love, the strongest emotion known to man,
Since the time of creation when the world began.
Man has sacrificed life and died for love,
A power so strong surely comes from above.

The love of a mother for her child,
The purest of all love can sometimes go wild,
As she tries to protect her kin from all harm,
Ever worrying and watching to raise the alarm.

The love of a young man for his bride,
Is as deep as the ocean and twice as wide.
Few faults, imperfections, can e'er be seen,
Love takes them to lands no one's ever been.

True love mellows with age like a fine old wine,
As the pair become closer their two hearts entwine.
The passion of youth is nearly all spent,
Now peace and harmony is their sole intent.

Delights of The Soil

L emons are juicy but so very sour,
O lives are oily, delicious at any hour,
V ictoria plums, served with thick, hot custard,
E lderberry wine with ham rolls and mustard.

T omatoes, eaten with onions and cheese,
H oney from busy bees is sure to please,
Y ams, tropical tubers are really delicious.

N uts which are crunchy and full of good oil,
E lderflower, a tonic grown in good soil,
I ris, a flower used for buttonholes by Bill,
G rapes taken to hospital when friends are ill,
H arricot beans, a good soup for tea,
B lackcurrants in tarts, full of vitamin 'C',
O nions add flavour to many good dishes,
U pside down fruit pudding meets everyone's wishes,
R edcurrants make jelly for that special treat.

A pples every day keeps the doctor away,
S trawberries and cream enjoyed on pay day.

T ulips bring joy when spring comes along,
H eather on mountains makes one burst into song,
Y ew trees produce dark leaves and red fleshy fruits,

S wede, disliked by some but others it suits,
E lm trees found on banks of rivers where we fish,
L eeks added to broth makes a lovely Welsh dish,
F ruits of the soil to be relished with good grace.

Questions

Why are we here asked my daughter one day,
I pondered the question, thought hard what to say.
We're just here to live life and prolong the race,
I looked at my child and saw her puzzled face.

Why do we laugh dad when we just want to cry,
I answered her query, giving it my best try.
Laughter makes people happy, then you don't feel sad,
Now surely my daughter that cannot be bad.

Why do we lie dad, sometimes even steal,
I tried hard to understand how she must feel.
We're not always good dear, but try not to worry,
Enjoy yourself poppet, don't grow up in a hurry.

Why did mam die dad and leave us alone,
I looked at my princess, said in measured tone.
'She died 'cause God loved her, longed to see her sweet face,
She's gone up to Heaven to reserve us a place.'

Laughter

Laughter is a beautiful sound,
It helps to make the world go round.
Sometimes life seems not worth living,
Then laughter's gift is worth giving.

Children's laughter playing in the park,
Teenagers giggling, having a lark.
Comics relating well known old jokes,
Brings tears from laughter to all old folks.

Much better to laugh to hide a sad heart,
Then people laugh with you and take part,
Your drawn into life, not thrown aside,
Laughter's been your saviour, sadness has died.

The Face of The Clown

Tear drops trickle down the face of the clown,
He looks dejected, his face creased in a frown.
Coco tries very hard to hide his sad heart,
Brightens up and makes ready to play his part.

He enters the ring as the children all cheer,
Coco juggles the balls and gets into gear.
He does acrobats, taking chance after chance,
Delighting the crowd with a skilled performance.

Coco's now feeling fine, he's worked out his grief,
His melancholy gone, it was very brief.
The audience give him their love and respect,
He now feels valued, making the right effect.

Transformations

Sunlight filtering through the woodland trees,
Creating a magic wonderland of dreams,
Where fairies live, dancing around toadstools,
And drinking dewdrops from dainty acorn cups.

Moonlight shining on the vast unchartered sea,
Creating a romantic atmospheric peace.
Persuading young lovers to open up their hearts,
And declare their undying love and devotion.

Companionship from man's best friend,
Creating love and fulfilling needs.
Giving a purpose to many folk's lives,
Helping the blind and assuaging the lonely.

Babies bathed and silently sleeping,
Creating feelings of love and wonder.
Nourishing our tired and jaded souls,
And bringing joy and hope for the future.

People

People populate the earth,
Every second giving birth.
Every colour, every size,
Some grow foolish, some grow wise.

People from all walks of life,
Most work hard, all face strife,
Keeping body and soul together,
Battling with all kinds of weather.

Children are my favourite people,
Growing tall just like a steeple.
Free of artifice and vice,
Some grow up to be real nice.

People can be cruel and cold,
Committing crimes evil and bold,
But tragedy brings out their best,
Then, surely they deserve to rest.

The Shires Retire

They'd worked really well in their lifetime together,
Pulling the barges in all winds and weather.
Up and down the canal with deliveries of coal,
Much better by far than a life on the dole.

Porgy and Bess were their names, they worked hard and long,
They were now getting old and were not quite so strong.
Their employer was kind, gave them plenty of oats,
For which they repaid Dan by pulling his boats.

After years of full labour Dan prospered well,
But never considered his horses to sell.
Bought a house in the dales with a big field nearby,
Where his faithful workmates could eat, sleep and lie.

The horses attuned to their new life of leisure,
But soon became bored with no work just pure pleasure.
After a lifetime of work they missed their routine,
So Dan brought in some children to brighten the scene.

In return for a fee the horses gave them a ride,
And Dan was quite happy with a bob on the side.
Now, retirement was a time when they all enjoyed life,
A life full of excitement with none of the strife.

The Pit Ponies

Their shift has now ended for the last time,
They enter the daylight, leave behind the grime.
They've worked long and hard for most of their life,
A life without pleasure, with plenty of strife.

Their eyes are unfocused, not used to the light,
Working in darkness has diminished their sight.
Their spirit broken by time spent underground,
Where the cold and the damp are equally found.

The past now behind them, the future looks bright,
Their working life over, they've now earned the right,
To retire to the country to live by the sea,
In an Animal Reserve with a luscious lea.

Their life has now changed, they're happy at last,
No drudgery now, that's all in the past.
Children visit the ponies each day after school,
Bring them sugar lumps and water, to keep them cool.

My Pet

My Yorkie is a source of pleasure,
The joy she gives beyond all measure.
She greets me in my darkest hour,
My life's renewed by her strange power.

We walk together in the park,
And listen to the joyful lark.
As we go forward side by side,
She fills my heart with so much pride.

My house no more a silent tomb,
Is full of life in every room.
Her toys and bones lie everywhere,
My life is now no longer bare.

Our Susie

The loss of dear Susie is so hard to bear,
It's the price of love, of giving your care.
Her time was up, we took her to the Vet,
She put her to sleep, our sweet little pet.

We carried her home, laid her on the table,
Fourteen years have gone by, it seems like a fable.
No more pain for Susie, resting under our lawn,
Our broken hearts ache, as we rise each dawn.

We think back to the time when we first brought her home,
She'd sneak out of the front door, she loved to roam.
We taught her to sit and run to command,
If she performed well, our love she'd demand.

Man's best friend is his dog, is a true saying,
For years of devotion, one has to start paying.
Try to think of the good times, the fun that you had,
With such wonderful memories, you mustn't feel sad.

Remembrance

Was he a coward or a really brave man?
Was he called Trevor or maybe just Dan?
One thing's for sure he belonged to the army,
He may have been Irish and come from Killarney.

When he was young was he really handsome?
Was he as brave as portrayed by Samson?
Did he flirt with the girls and kiss more than one,
Or did he drink with his mates when his workday was done?

Did he love his mum and be loyal to his dad?
Did he cry at films and sometimes feel sad?
Did he have a wife and a wee baby boy,
Worshipped by his mum who named him Leroy?

Was he a loner or a gregarious man?
Did he have a hero and become his best fan?
This unknown soldier would now have been old,
But sadly his true story will never be told.

A Prayer for The Past

She looks at the picture displayed on the wall,
The arrangement of flowers makes her recall,
Fields abundant with poppies growing in France,
Her melancholy eyes light up and dance.

She thinks of her lover, a Frenchman so strong,
Their love was consuming, carried them along.
They cared not for the future, nor the distant past,
A love so demanding couldn't possibly last.

They lay midst the daises and poppies so red,
Within two short years her lover was dead.
He died for his country, along with their love,
The futility of war witnessed from above.

The scene has now changed, she sees poppies falling,
In honour of her love, obeying his calling.
She wishes he'd survived to make her his wife,
But thanks God for their love that's enriched her life.

The Other Side of The Pane

He looked through the window at the food on the table,
Sat down on a stool was a young girl called Mabel.
The table was laden with a lavish spread,
Jim was hungry and sad now his parents were dead.

Mabel looked at the orphan and turned up her nose,
Spoilt and indulged it was her favourite pose.
Touched by a tear welling up in his eye,
She opened the window and passed him a pie.

He gobbled it up, gave his thanks and moved on,
Mabel called him back, her disdain now all gone.
"Come on in and sit down and eat all you can,
You need to fill out well before you're a man."

He ate lots of peaches and a huge fresh cream cake,
Jim confided in Mabel that his mum used to bake.
They laughed and chatted and became real good mates,
And made plans for a good many more future dates.

The Old Soldier

The café was full apart from two seats,
It was a venue where all folk used to meet.
A very old man entered and we both sat at the table,
He positioned his crutch as neat as he was able.

We ordered our meal and started to eat,
He mopped his brow, overcome with the heat.
'It's the pain you know, it's really a pest,
It's a World War 1 wound and it gives me no rest.'

It was now 1995, so he must have been ninety-nine,
And a story for my paper would have been fine.
'Would you tell me about your war life' I asked bravely.
'Never talk about the horrors' he replied very gravely.

'I'd like to tell you a story that's really worthwhile,
It was one minute past midnight,' he related with style.
'Christmas Day had arrived and both sides laid down their arms.
They hugged, laughed and cried which was a great balm.

Rolled up paper made a ball which we kicked about,
Stories were told which no soldier did doubt.
Photos were shown and families discussed,
Men's faces were changed as we kicked the dust.
We started to sing hymns and carols we all knew,
And as voices combined our confidence grew.

After eating and singing we slept on the floor,
We woke to the sound of gunfire once more,
The horrors of war had once more begun,
But Christmas Day memories would last till all fighting was done.'

'Thank-you for telling me such an uplifting story,
With no talk of injuries which can be so gory.
Every Christmas I'll think of that day and how fighting did cease,
And pray that one day this world will find peace.'

A Lullabye

Sleep little baby while you can,
One day you'll grow to be a man,
With work and tasks to fill your day,
No more able to rest and lay.

Sleep little baby while you can,
One day you'll grow to be a man.
You'll have a fine job in the city,
And maybe you'll become quite witty.

Sleep little baby while you can,
One day you'll grow to be a man.
You'll have a house and maids and servants,
Your grand lifestyle will keep you fervent.

Sleep little baby while you can,
One day you'll grow to be a man.
Your children will grow to be a credit,
Your house and cars be out of debit.

Sleep little baby while you can,
One day you'll grow to be a man.
Your life's ambitions will all be fired,
You'll then relax, become retired.

Memories

Memories, with age, become more dear,
And looking back allays the fear,
That comes in time to everyone,
When all life's tasks are nearly done.

Blowing out the birthday candles,
Wearing pretty coloured bangles.
Thoughts like that bring childhood back,
Make up for all the things one lacks.

Schools had forty children in a class,
Some worked hard and gained a pass,
Going on to higher learning,
Keeping life's ambitions burning.

Sunday was a day of rest,
Maybe kids became a pest.
They had to go to Sunday School,
To keep dad's temper down real cool.

When I think of times gone past,
I do regret they cannot last.
One must look forward every day,
To keep sad thoughts and fears at bay.

Our Library

Our cultural centre is in Cwmbran,
Where all can visit, including your gran.
It's pleasant and clean with comfortable seating,
In winter the library has central heating.

To join the library you don't have to pay,
Which is a bonus at the end of the day.
Books are free, CD's, DVD's, lent at low cost,
And the internet's free, when one feels at a loss.

The shelves are furnished with thousands of books,
Written by fine authors and a few famous cooks.
They write about love, life and exciting travels,
Which twist and turn as the story unravels.

They cater for children with facts and with fiction,
Reading each day helps to improve their diction.
Tots of two can arrive in a real paddy,
But the books calm them down when read by their daddy.

The young and the old work on the computers,
Finding out truths to appease the disputers.
Some struggle with two fingers to find out the facts,
While dramatists quickly type out their acts.

The staff at our library are so obliging,
The queries they cope with are rather surprising.
On computers they look for the book you require,
They search till they find the one you desire.

Our libraries are a fine institution,
Part of our heritage and constitution.
They're a haven of peace to read during leisure,
Providing knowledge and giving us pleasure.

Thoughts in The Night

My favourite time is the still of the night,
Where my thoughts give expression away from the light.
I dream of a life full of love with no pain,
Where folk work to their potential with no thought of gain.
Where flowers would bloom and ne'er fade away,
And the sun would keep shining day after day.
Our cattle would live without fear of slaughter,
And men would love and cherish our daughters.
Our children would play and learn by example,
They'd never be cold and their food would be ample.
Bullies would reform, no more to rise up,
All children would thrive, drink from the same loving cup.

I think of this life and I wish I could change,
Certain aspects of life in the past re-arrange,
But this journey we take is not a rehearsal,
Whatever we do there is no reversal.
You just have to go forward, do the best that you can,
And hope that in so doing you'll become a 'New Man'.

A Christmas Melody

Christmas time is here once more,
Celebrated by rich and poor.
Julie hangs her stocking up,
She's praying for a little pup,
A little pup. A little pup.

The day's arrived, no dog has come,
A pair of silver skates from mum.
But wait, what's in that big round dish,
It looks just like a little fish.
A little fish. A little fish.

Johnny Davies wants a fish,
Maybe I'll change it for my wish.
I'll raid his house making no bustle,
And change it for his small Jack Russell.
His small Jack Russell. His small Jack Russell.

Christmas Day

Church bells chime on Christmas Day,
As the congregation sing and pray.
The Priest relates the story of Christ's birth,
Then we sing carols for all our worth.

After church we go home for Christmas dinner,
This wonderful meal is yet another winner.
Mum has a rest while we do the dishes,
Then we play charades which meets everyone's wishes.

For tea we have a festive spread,
With cakes and tarts and home-made bread.
After all that food we need a good walk,
So we take the dog and enjoy a long talk.

As we scramble home snowflakes start falling,
As we clamber o'er fields and dry stone walling,
Laughing and joking and happily singing,
This special day ends with church bells ringing.

Christmases Past

Christmas time spent long ago,
Meant holly, friends and mistletoe.
Singing carols all together,
Often in inclement weather.

Stockings hung up overnight,
Opened long before 'twas light.
Searching in the toe young Jenny,
Found a sparkling, bright new penny.

Christmas dinner 'round the table,
One leg being quite unstable.
Aunty Pearl and Uncle Billy,
Paper hats on looking silly.

Dad stood up and carved the turkey,
Everyone then feeling perky.
Sprouts and spuds and crispy pork,
And afterwards a good brisk walk.

At tea we had a festive feed,
Then played charades and disagreed.
A good sing song ended the day,
With hot drinks brought in on a tray.

A Prayer for Peace

Peace to the world at Christmas time,
I hope you like this little rhyme.
It is the birthday of God's son,
So celebrate, have lots of fun.

Eat, drink and have a jolly time,
Listen to the church bells chime.
Sing carols 'round the Christmas tree,
Let all your inhibitions free.

But don't forget the other side,
It was for this that Jesus died.
To save the world from vice and sin,
Try not to let the devil win.

Printed in Great Britain
by Amazon.co.uk, Ltd.,
Marston Gate.